WTF!

WHY PARENTS SHOULD NEVER TEXT!

BLACK & WHITE PUBLISHING

First published 2015
by Black & White Publishing Ltd
29 Ocean Drive, Edinburgh EH6 6JL

1 3 5 7 9 10 8 6 4 2   15 16 17 18

ISBN: 978 1 84502 992 0

Design and arrangement © Black & White Publishing 2015

The publisher has made every reasonable effort to contact copyright
holders. Any errors are inadvertent and anyone who for any reason
has not been contacted is invited to write to the publisher so that a full
acknowledgment can be made in subsequent editions of this work.

A CIP catalogue record for this book is available from the British Library.

Typeset by 3btype.com
Printed and bound by Nørhaven, Denmark

Contents

Text Message   Send

Dad

How do u work this iMessage program? How's the

Dad ur on the toilet...

That's why I'm smiling!

Text Message　Send

DAD

Dad

There is lightly fried fish fillets for dinner

Dad it's 1.15am wtf

Do you want the lightly fried fish fillets or not?

Well I mean yea

OK thought so come on downstairs they're still hot

Wait what did you just make them?

Yes I wasn't tired so I decided to make some lightly fried fish fillets

Say lightly fried fish fillets one more time dad...

Text Message   Send

Dad

Come over and mount my penis today

please

plasma

i hit wrong key

Text Message | Send

Dad

Youre 65 today! Happy birthday!!!

How do you feel??

Another day closer to Velcro strapons

What? Strap ons? Um?

Velcro sneakers. This phone is messed up.

Text Message | Send

Dad
Dad do you have any idea where my certificate is?
it's in your mother's anus
anus
ANUS
Uh...?
in her anus
jesus mary and joseph upstairs in her house in storage
Wow. Ok I will search mums anus. Thanks dad.
Text Message
Send

Dad

You want us to cook anything special for Easter?

i will eat anything

but your mum and i have not stopped talking about your dick since we had it at Christmas

so juicy

Juicy Easter dick. Got it.

Wow. I'm afraid to ask what you want for dessert.

Text Message   Send

Dad

Don't come home me and your mum are getting it on tonight

HAHAHA autocorrect, right?

What do you mean

You made a typo ... look at your last text

No I did not make a typo

?!*?*!....

Text Message Send

Dad
Hey whats up?
Gas prices
Lol dad. I meant like what are you doing?
Your mum
I want to move out
Text Message
Send

Dad
I'm hungry!
Hi Hungry, nice to meet you. I'm Dad.
DAD! I'm serious!
I thought your name was hungry?
ARE YOU KIDDING ME!?
No, I'm Dad...
Text Message
Send

Dad
You look guilty
Did you eat mum's coochie?
Ew definitely not.
Her chocolate coochie
Dad mum's white.
her chocolate cookie. Don't be an idiot.
No. I didn't eat her chocolate cookie.
k
Text Message
Send

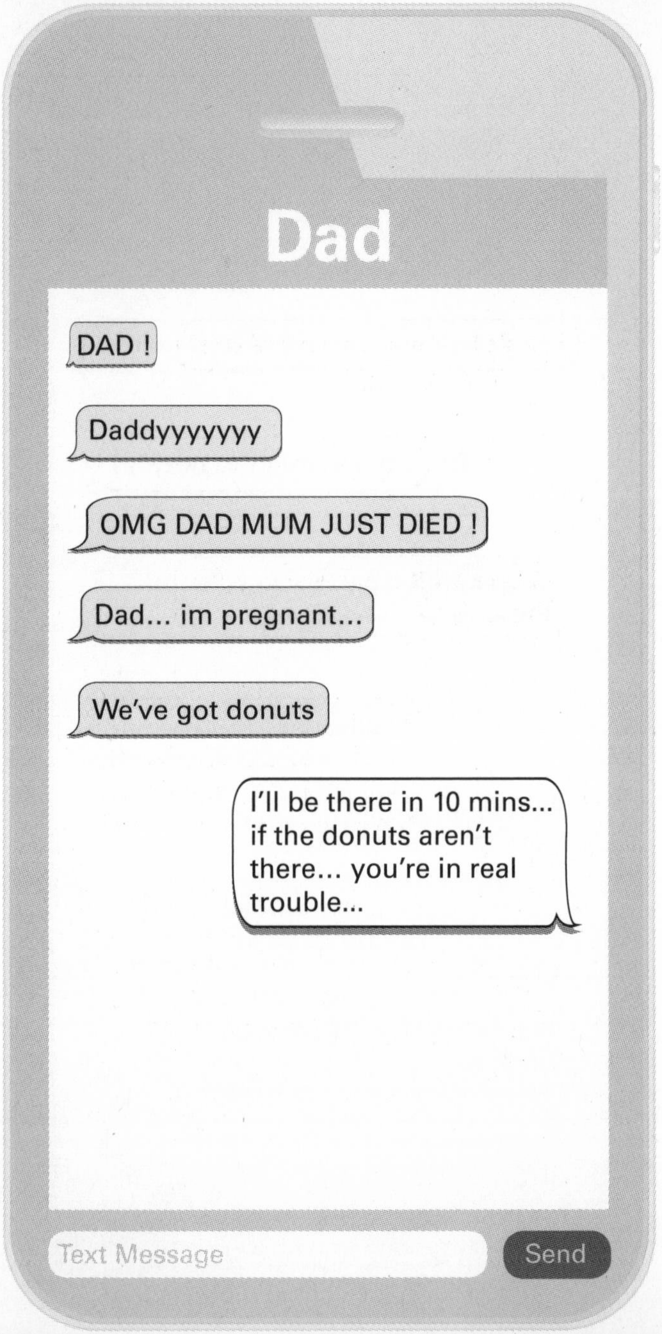
Dad
DAD !
Daddyyyyyyy
OMG DAD MUM JUST DIED !
Dad... im pregnant...
We've got donuts
I'll be there in 10 mins... if the donuts aren't there... you're in real trouble...
Text Message
Send

Dad

I can't believe you're a texter!

I am starting to like it...

You're a little excessive with the '...'s :p

Thank you for bringing this to my attention and I will cease immediately.

Text Message | Send

Dad

If you and your girlfriend want to come over for dinner, be here at 6

I'm grilling up some baby black kids. Should be delicious.

As tempting as that sounds we both have to work late

Yea I meant baby back ribs. All the more for me.

Lol enjoy

Text Message

Send

Dad

Your perfume came in the post today. I sprayed it all over my body and now I smell like a cookie.

WTF Dad?

I'm keeping it.

Ok.....

Text Message

Send

Dad
Whats for dinner?
Im gonna hunt you down and slice your throat and drink your blood while I rip your legs off and cook them over an open fire slowly while watching you squirm...
WHAT THE FUCK DAD!?
Oops! sorry! Stupid auto correct! I meant "Steak and mashed potatoes". I love you honey :D
Im going out for dinner tonight
Text Message
Send

Dad

> What is a redheaded ninja?

Eh?

> What is a redheaded ninja?

I don't know

> Ginja

Really dad...really???

Text Message | Send

Dad

Honey, your mum and I are going to a vagina. We left money in the drawer for your food.

WTF DAD??!?!?!?!???!!!

Sorry, I mean vacuum*

OMFG I MASTURBATE VACATION* !!!!!

Shut. What the hull is wrong with this phone. I *****mean***** ****vacation***. No busses over.

Duck. You know what i mean. No boys. I need a new phone. I hate this auto-cucumber!

Text Message   Send

Dad

Jenny's rabbit died last night so we went to the pet shop and bought an almost identical one. Wondering if she's going to notice.

OMG WTF DAD

You could have told me the truth

Sorry honey meant for Uncle Mark.

I would have noticed

I had a £20 bet with mum you wouldn't.

Text Message   Send

Dad

Are we getting together next Sunday for Father's Day?

No way

I'm spending it with my other children

There's always next year

Text Message   Send

Dad

How is practice going?

Terrible I want to stab everybody here

Okay just don't get any blood on your clothes

You're a police officer you shouldn't be condoning this

Don't tell me how to live my life

Text Message   Send

Dad
Dad there's a moth on the outside of the bathroom door can you get rid of it?
Pls hurry because I'm going to cry
Dad
Dad
Dad is dead. You're next. Love, Moth
Text Message
Send

TECHNOLOGY

Mum

Gotnewphoneanddontknowwhere spacebaris!

I told mawmawifyourplaneislateor uaretootiredwewontbethere

Figured out spacebar

Text Message   Send

Mum

人

方土错日

Why are you texting in Chinese?? Lol!

然

!!!!!!!!!!!

木弟戈

LMAO. you got stuck in chinese mode didn't you?

!!!!!!!!!!

Text Message

Send

TECHNOLOGY

Mum

Hi Bridget I space space space space how space are space you space doing period capital eye love this new phone exclamation point

I see youre using voice text. You don't have to say space mum it does it for you

I cucumber letter pea Ritalin

What? Mum stop just type

Text Message   Send

Mum

I think there's something wrong with my phone. I don't think my texts are going through.

Yeah, they're getting through.

[Delivered]

How can you be sure?

Text Message   Send

Dad

Goon

Good

First

Never mind. Thought I was on google.

Text Message   Send

Mum
How make chicken
what
Where buy chicken
mum this isn't google
Avocado
Text Message
Send

Mum

I think I keep getting messages or missed calls or something.

From who?

Some woman named...Betty Low...

Uhm, BATTERY LOW?!?!

YEAH THAT'S IT!!

Text Message

Send

Mum

could you ring my phone please? I can't remember where it is...

mum, what are you doing right now?

looking for my phone, why?

OMG, YOU ARE TEXTING ME! YOU TEXT WITH A PHONE! THE PHONE IS IN YOUR HAND!

Ooh yes, thanks sweetie ☺

-.-

Text Message   Send

Mum

If I searched for a picture of Johnny depps butt how do I erase the search? I don't want dad to see

Text Message   Send

Mum

Are you and your boyfriend all right??

Yes were fine !! Why do you ask??

Oh well I heard you screaming "Die you fat evil pig"...

Mum I wasn't breaking up with him I was playing Angry Birds...

Text Message   Send

Mum

im eating lunch now. TWITTER.

im going to sit in the sun now. TWITTER.

what are you doing?

tweeting its fun

OMG putting 'TWITTER' at the back of a text message doesn't mean you're tweeting...

PS: my daughter sucks. TWITTER.

Text Message

Send

Dad
Burn off the boobies
DAD!!!!! WTFFFF!!!!!!!!!
Just got your message. I told Siri to say to you, turn off heater pls. Showed mum, she laughed her heart out.
Text Message
Send

Dad
Hey son! Which phone do you like most? Samsung S3 or iphone 6?
OMG DAD!!! I LIKE THE S3! OMG THANKS DAD!!!
It’s not for you. Its for your sister.
Text Message
Send

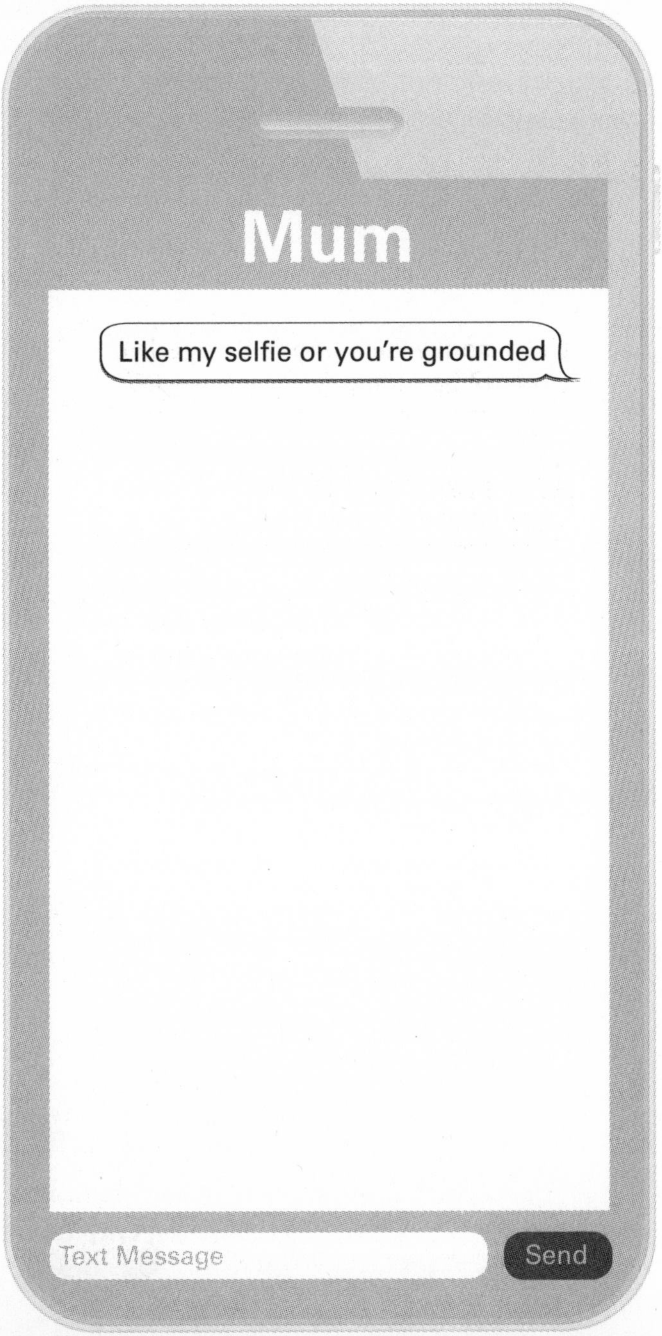
Mum
Like my selfie or you're grounded
Text Message
Send

Mum

I can do this without typing

Fine

Daddy just told me that all I have to do is press the microphone button and it will type it into me and I like that it was it's done done and send

Oh my god this is so cool I don't even have to type cool hit done and send

Hey did you guys know that you didn't have to type it all you had to do was say it

Yes it's been that way for years.

Oh my god this is so much fun

UBI a motherfucker

What?

What Bruce Willis says it is dye had movies

Good night

Lou Lou Skip to my moon

What is happening?

Text Message   Send

Mum

I'll talk to you later my phone's dying

Of what?

Cancer, Mum. My phone is dying of cancer. -_-

Text Message   Send

Mum

Did you send my stuff yet?

Sorry, I can't hear you. I think we have a bad connection. Try again later.

Muuuummmm that doesn't work with texts.

Text Message   Send

Dad

WTF???? You have herpes?!? Why the hell didn't you tell me before it was too late to get condoms.

O.0

Don't gimmie that bullshit!!! what will happen if my wife finds out?

Ummmmmm...... hi dad

50" flatscreen, xbox 360, or £1000?

All and a door lock w/ a subscription to brazzers

Text Message   Send

RELATIONSHIPS

Dad

I'm gay

Im not gay your mother took my phone

Text Message   Send

Dad
I just heard Amanda moved back to town
As in your ex Amanda?
Yep. That's the one.
Maybe one day you'll cum into her.
Hahhaha been there done that dad.
That was supposed to say run.
Text Message
Send

Dad

Anything else exciting going on this week?

No not really

Mum's got a bad cold.

She's spreading her legs at work.

So that's how she got that raise. Hahahaha

Germs

She doesn't spread her legs for anyone. Trust me I know.

Text Message

Send

Dad
Hey you want to come over tonight again?
I'm pregnant
Haha jokes yes I'll come over
Babe?
Hello?
Hello this is Rick's mother he fainted about 5 minutes ago the ambulance is here any idea why he fainted?
Text Message
Send

Mum

Hey John I'll be waiting 2 fuck you tonight

Ummmm mum? Something u want 2 tell me? Dads name is Rick

Oops I was mmmm joking

Oops baby it was so funny I just asked my daughter 2 fuck instead of u

Still me mum

Oh

Text Message
Send

Dad

> come on down, dinner is ready

Be there in a min, I'm doing Lauren.

> who the fuck is lauren

> if she is your girlfriend, she can have some dinner too.

Dad! I meant laundry. I'm not a lesbian.

> that's a shame. men are dicks. Now come and eat

Text Message | Send

Dad
Do you need anything from the shops?
Some condoms. going out w/some girls... I need protection
Son
Yessssss??
Your face is protection enough.
...
Text Message
Send

Mum
Hey babe! Ready to get down 2night?
Young man! This is Susan's mother! She left her phone home
Uh oh......
HAHA! Got you biotch! Now tell me what were doin again 2night?
Yea we gonna do it so hard you won't be able 2 get outta bed in the mornin!
I was kidding... I'm really her mother and I'm calling your mum.
Text Message
Send

TEXT SPEAK

Mum

The road was a little icy out today. Be careful when you drive.

I will.

YOLO.

It's usually not meant as a warning, Mum.

Text Message   Send

Mum
I'm learning how to hashtag!
That's great, Mum.
Hashtag conversation with son.
Text Message
Send

Mum

> Your great aunt just passed away. LOL

Why is that funny?

> It's not funny! What do you mean?

Mum lol means laughing out loud!

> Oh my goodness!! I sent that to everyone I thought it meant lots of love. I have to call everyone back oh god

Text Message　　　　Send

Mum
"What does IDK, LY & TTYL mean?"
I don't know, love you, talk to you later.
OK, I will ask your sister.
Text Message
Send

Mum

When are you coming home?

Hello? WTF??

Mum! Do you know what that means?

Yeah, are you coming home Wednesday, Thursday or Friday?

Nope. Not what that means.

Mum
Got an A in Chemistry!!
WTF, well done!
Mum, what do you think WTF means?
Well That's Fantastic
Text Message
Send

Mum

Waiting for her right now

Cool beans

Let's keep the "cool beans" down to a minimum

Warm beans ?

Let's just not use the word beans. Like ever.

Cool frijoles

Text Message   Send

When r u going 2 b home?

Later we're at a movie

When does the movie end?

Idk

What does Idk mean?

I don't know

U sent it

It means I don't know!!!!!!!!!!

Ok

Text Message   Send

TEXT SPEAK

Mum
You know I just figured out what OMG meant – what the heck is ttyl?
talk to you later
Oh...thought it was like tiny tits you loser!
Text Message
Send

Dad

Hi, I am fairly new to Facebook. Mind accepting my friend request?

you made a facebook? WTF!!

What does "WTF" mean?

oh it means welcome to facebook

Text Message   Send

Mum

<3 for dinner

Yes I always love dinner.

Doesn't that mean ice cream?

Text Message   Send

Mum
wht r u dng fr smr brk if th trp ges cnclld?
Mum what on earth are you trying to say? Those aren’t words.
Text Message
Send

Mum
Are u going to have dinner
No I'm not. I'm so proud of you texting me
Igots goode tets
Never mind.
Text Message
Send

Dad
Dad, can I ask you something?
Ffs
What?
Feel free son
Dad...... ffs means for fucks sake.
...oh
Text Message
Send

Mum

Ok it does t t sggm Bhoaqamaosiq

?

Lol lol i fell asleep texting

Hahaha

Text Message | Send

Mum
LOL
GAGS
omggg
Go and Get stuffed
Gags
I worked with a guy who signed his notes to me with that, instead of yours faithfully
Text Message
Send

Mum

({}) sweetie What's this?

Uhm.... Why do you ask

Well because Joanne text me it and said your skirt was too short last Friday and that your entire ({}) was out

Mum, call her a bitch and delete her as a contact

Why?

Because she just said my entire lady part was out

EMOJI

Text Message   Send

Mum

> You want chocolate chips in all the pancakes right

> Yes yes yes

> Mum those are poop not chocolate chips

> I forgot!! Why does poop have such a cute face.

Text Message | Send

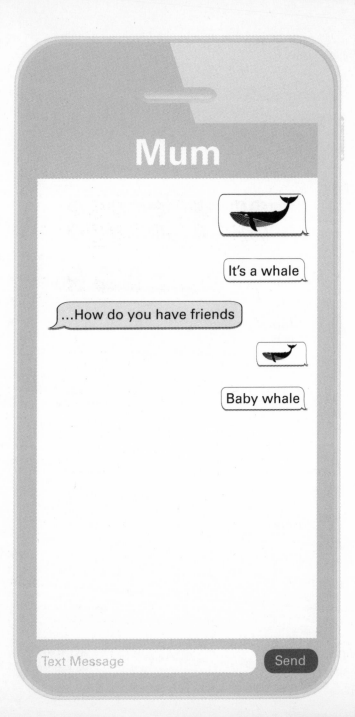

Mum

Mum

You are my 🌍

Mum

I learned how to make a little face with typing!

Yeah, that's been around for a while.

"}+

What is THAT!?

It's a winky face.

Text Message   Send

Mum

> Hey hun, what does this mean??? (.)(.)

o.O in what context

> Im in love with your (.)(.)

Eheheh; Eyes mum. Dad loves your eyes.

> Awe that cute. Thank you =D

Be sure to tell him you enjoy his 8===D Smile

Text Message   Send

Mum

> Can you please call me when you need to be picked up! Don't do anything stupid! :-)8

What is that emoticon?

> Bowtie man! He doesn't do anything stupid.

Text Message · Send

Mum

K:(

What's on its head?

It has flat hair, bad hair day.

Text Message　　Send

Mum

Why the happy poop mum

What? No! That is a burnt marshmallow

no mum

Isnt it

its happy poop

Why happy poop ever

I don't know

Text Message   Send

EMOJI

Mum

 LOL couldn't find lips so I thought this octopus was cute

Text Message | Send

Mum

Are u sore

Do ducks have jackets

Did muck save maggots

Ughhhh

Does husk make gaggles

Never mind

what

what...I just..what.

Text Message   Send

MUM

Mum

> Please don't text me for the next hour, I'm going to be on the treadmill.

I wasn't planning on texting you.

> What did I just say?

Text Message | Send

Mum

I packed you lunch today, it's in the fridge

Thanks ma

You are welcome.

Do not shake your dick or it will explode everywhere

I mean, your drink. It is very carbonated.

Lol. Ok mum I won't.

Text Message

Send

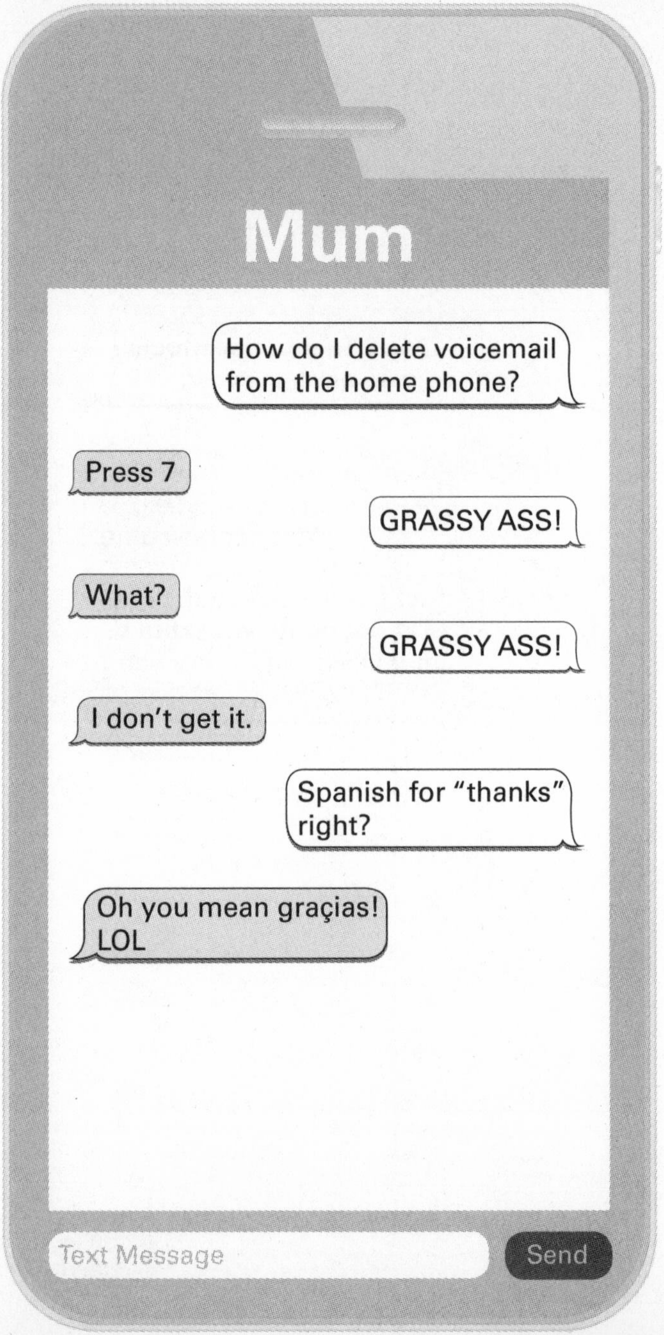
Mum
How do I delete voicemail from the home phone?
Press 7
GRASSY ASS!
What?
GRASSY ASS!
I don't get it.
Spanish for "thanks" right?
Oh you mean graçias! LOL
Text Message
Send

Mum

Don't do too much today. Stay home and rest.

I left orange juice and chicken soup in the fridge.

And put tissues by the bed in case you needs to blow your load.

Love mum

Text Message   Send

Mum

Andy.

Andy.

Andy.

Andy.

Andy.

Andy.

Andy.

Andy.

Andy.

Andy.

Mum! What!?

Well if you're going to be a big grumpus, never mind!

Text Message | Send

Mum

There is cum all in my hair... Thanks to your brother, he is so grounded!!

OMG WHAT!?

He got cum in my hair. "mummy look what I can do" GOD!

Mum please look back at what you wrote...

OMG I MEANT GUM HE BLEW A BUBBLE AND IT DROPPED IT MY HAIR! I SWEAR!

HAHAHAHAHAHAHAHA-HAHA oh my life is messed up...

Text Message   Send

Mum

[27/04 12.03PM]

Coll mum!!!!!!!

[6.04PM]

Call mum!!!!!

[8.07PM]

Call mum . Call mum !!!!!!!!

[28/04 1.54PM]

Call mum !!!!

[1.54PM]

Call mum . Call mum !!!!!

[2.54PM]

Call mum !!!

[2.54PM]

Call mum !!!

[5.06PM]

Call mum !!!!!! Coll mum !!!

[9/05 11.31AM]

Call mum !!! Now !!

Text Message.

Send

Mum

Mum did u buy cream cheese

Yes

And crackers?

No I guess we r crackalaking lol

Mum stop

Text Message   Send

Mum

At what age does Ryan Gosling have to change his name to Ryan Goose?

Text Message | Send

Mum

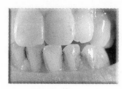

Is that your teeth?!

Absolutely

Text Message   Send

Mum

Should I just make macaroni and cheese?

Your home?

My home what?

Your at home?

My at home what?

Look u little shit...

Text Message   Send

Mum

I need more contacts. I just put in my last pair. So I'll need another set in like a month and a half if that's possible.

Sure - - do u order them or should eye?

Text Message Send

Mum

Mum. Where are you????

Leaving tesco. Halfway home. Why sweetie?

You took me to tesco with you -.-

OH DAMN! Be there in a bit

Text Message | Send

Mum
Mum, how do you have NO WRINKLES?! And I have some already!?
I avoided wrinkles by never smiling at kids.
Explains our childhood.
Text Message
Send

Mum

Hey, I'm really angry, mum

Oh, should I cheer you up?

Duh.

You are my sunshine, my only sunshine. You make me happy, when skies are grey, ...

Actually, I was thinking more on the lines of buying me something expensive...

How about you just stay angry, ok?

Text Message

Send

Mum

Are you coming to johns company picnic on Monday?

Yep! I'll be there, and so will my famous striptease!

No one wants to see that mum!!!! Lol.

Stripsteak! Yum yum yum

Yum in my bum!

TUM!!!! Yikes.

And you were making fun of me?

Text Message   Send

Mum
Did you leave yet?
No, I'm still downstairs fondling the landlady.
WHAT?
Fondling the laundry
Folding the landlady downstairs. Got it?
This was a great chat.
Text Message
Send

Mum

I just suckled nervous boobs week!

Omg what??

I ate this new phone..... signed up for nervous blast week*

Netflix last week **

Hahahahahahaha omg mum that made my day lmao

Text Message

Send

Mum

Need me to bring anything for dinner? Or dessert?

No! But when you get here I need you to put new batteries in my cameltoe.

I can't figure out how to do it.

In your WHAT!!!

In my camera! What is a cameltoe?

Lol don't even ask mum.

Oh God I googled it!

Text Message
Send

Mum
Does dad have shoes for the wedding?
Yes, he has brown ones.
Brown? Do they match his outfit?
Well his pubes are grey, so... I'd say yes.
LMFAO what does that matter! Is he going naked? Hahahahaha
Suit! Oh God!
Text Message
Send

Mum

My Mum is the BIGGEST fucking bitch in the whole god damn world I hope she burns in hell for this shit.

IKR what a slut

LOL right????? She can suck my dick

Ohhh you mean that little tic-tac?

Huh?

Get your ass home.

Text Message   Send

Mum

Do u want a chicken

Respond ASAP

Do I want a chicken?
Like a live one?

No died

Is it dead?

Yes

Ok...

For eating right?

Come down stair now

Text Message Send

Dad
I heard mum got stung by a few bees this morning. Is she ok??? Hospital???
She is okay now. No hospital.
She had to take the deep penis.
Uh... What?
I had to inject her with an EPIC PENIS.
Oh for Christ's sake.
Epi Pen
Text Message
Send

Dad

Busy dad?

No, just finished vacuuming

That hooker you left here has some serious sucking power.

DAD! LMAO I think you meant "Hoover"

Anyway do you want to go grab dinner?

I can't believe that just happened. I thought those auto corrects were fake.

Text Message   Send

Dad
You hungry dad?
Yeah I want your mums vagina
EWWWW
I meant lasagne, but I want that too ;)
Text Message
Send

Dad

Well I miss you and mum and can't wait to visit!

We miss you too and are keeping busy.

Well I just got hard and now I'm going to hop in the shower. We will see you tomorrow.

Dad! WTF? was it absolutely vital for you to tell me that?????

Oh wow. I meant I got Hardees burgers. For dinner. That sounded really bad.

Text Message | Send

Dad

Can you help me with my truck

Can't. your mother clogged up her vagina with hair again.

Um, what?

She never cleans it and it's all clogged up

Dad why are you telling me this? Come on man.

lol I meant her vacuum. The bagless one that she clogs up 4x a month.

Text Message   Send

Mum

Great news!!!! I finally found my GSPOT.

Um, Wow. Thank you so much for sharing. Congratulations?

I found it in the back seat of of my car.

Ok mum now this is just getting too weird. I know we are close but come on.

Huh?

Oh God! My GPS! Hahaha!!!

Text Message   Send

Mum

The cat wants to know why she found condoms in the laundry.

Text Message   Send

Mum
What did you do today mum
Cleaned, paid bills, made pasta
I just gave your father a huge boner and now he's passed out on the couch.
EW!!! do not need to know that!!!!!
Oh my goodness. I gave him a huge bowl. I'm laughing out loud.
I'm glad you are coz I want to barf.
Text Message
Send

Mum
I just found a pic of you holding your blueballs!
You were so adorable!
I don't recall ever taking that picture mum!!!
Please reread that msg
I wrote boombox! What is a blueball?
Ask dad
Text Message
Send

Dad
Done all your homework?
No, I've been masturbating. Why is it so much fun?
IDK son, I had the same problem too when I was younger.
Huh, I wonder if it was genetics.
Wait... I meant procrastinating.
Well, that's awkward.
Text Message
Send

Mum
Father's Day is coming and I just overheard your dad say he wants a new dick
A new dick
He said he wants a new dick
shit dick
A new shit dick. Got it. Thanks mum!
I am calling you.
Why didn't you answer?
Text Message
Send

Mum
Hi Dave, I found some cum on me and your fathers bed, what where you and lisa doing in our room? Love, mum.
OMG, im sooooooo sorry you found out this way! omg im so sorry mum!
I meant gum... What HAVE you been doing??
Can we talk later?
Text Message
Send

Mum

Hello Mr Lewis, this is Connie, tyler's mum. Just making sure we are still on for tonight's parent teacher conference.

Hi Connie. Yes, we're still on. I will come fuck you at 7. Speak soon.

Connie, I sincerely apologize. I meant to write "I will come find you at 7." That was my phone's autocorrect.

I am incredibly sorry.

Wow ok.

Text Message   Send

Dad

You're 16, sex doesn't exist for you. It's not real, like the Easter Bunny.

And you are married, it doesn't exist for you either. Ha.

Touché Son. Touché

Text Message | Send

Dad

> No sex, drugs, or alcohol tonight. Be safe.

I'm always safe. Because safe sex is great sex, better wear a latex.

> Knock that shit off right now!

Don't be jealous because I can have fun and youre married at home watching tv on a Friday night.

> Obviously I didn't raise you right...

Text Message

Send

Dad

How was your physical. Everything ok?

Doc said I have high cholesterol.

How do you lower it

Have to eat healthier and work out

No more buttsex for me!

Make that butter....

Text Message | Send

Mum

Come over if you can

Dad's outside trying to fuck the mailbox and it isn't pretty.

What the hell are you talking about

Just what I said

Fix the mailbox! Oh my God! Not the other thing!

Haha ok I can't be there til 2

Text Message | Send

DRINKING (AND DRUGS)

Mum

You are definitely coming here for Christmas right? I am cooking ham.

Yes – and I'm bringing drugs.

Oh like hell you are.

Don't you even THINK about bringing drugs into this house Melissa.

Wow chill mum. I meant I'm bringing DOUG.

Well why didn't you say that.

Text Message　　Send

Mum

Got 2 grams for $40

nvm wrong person

2 grams of what??

DANIEL ANSWER ME

Grammar books

Oh I thought you were talking about the weed lol

Did you have enough money or do you need me to put some more in your account?

A little more wouldn't hurt

Text Message | Send

DRINKING (AND DRUGS)

Mum

How did dads dr. appointment go?

Okay. He has heartburn. Doctor prescribed prostitutes.

2x per day

Wow. In that case I have heartburn too. Lol

Best prescription ever!

Oh gosh. Not funny. Prilosec. That is my worst auto correct ever!

Text Message   Send

Mum

Why is there a plastic bag sticking out of your back pack

Have u been buying drugs at school

hey can you do me a favour & open the bag

I don't want to know what's in it come home

It's going to hurt me to see what's in the bag I don't want u to be doing drugs

open the damn bag

I did

what's in it

Pretzels

I am sorry

Text Message

Send

Dad
hello heather I m a cute young man would u like 2 engage in underage drinking and mayb drugs??
Dad i know that's you
no i am a attractive teenage boy who has alcohol lets get crank
crunk
Dad you didn't even block your number
Text Message
Send

Mum
Am I too late for dinner?
Nope hurry up we just sharted and dad got high!
Dad got HIGH?! And who sharted?
Started and dad got hibachi.
Text Message
Send

Mum

What do you and Trisha want for Sunday dinner?

Chicken Pot Pie

What type of Pie? And where do I get pot?

What??

Mark, I don't know if I can buy POT legally.

Mum. Chicken pot pie. Not chicken, pot and pie. Call me.

Text Message

Send

Mum
What train will u get?
2.45 :-/
Guess u will have to get a glass of wine at the station to warm up
That bar closed!!
Fuck that
I know!
Text Message
Send

Mum

[25/04 10AM]

Woo hoooooo !!!!!

[26/04 10PM]

Hey sorry I was at happy hour

Text Message   Send

Mum

Sometimes I squat on the floor and put my arms around my knees and lean forward

Are you drunk

No. That's how I roll.

Bahahahahahaha!

Go to sleep

Text Message

Send

Mum

Heard you guys got drunk

heard you used to sell cocaine

Loved it too

Wernt no shame in my game

Text Message

Send

Mum
Where r u
On the streets
Doing what
Sellin dope
R u coming home soon we want ice creams. U should have money from your dope sales
Hahahahahaha
Text Message
Send

Dad
I'm in family room. Bring me a beer please.
Uh Dad...I'm still away for another week.
I'll wait.
Text Message
Send

Mum
Reached a new low. Drinking wine from my thermos while on the stair master.
Text Message
Send

Dad

It is 10pm where are you?

I am in a dark alley with my drug dealer trying to get a good deal on his new batch of weed

As long as I know where you are.

Text Message | Send

Dad
What you doing tonight
Studying
You are a nerd!!!
Get out there
Get drunk!!
You are ruining my name
At least pretend your
drunk in front of your
friends
Text Message
Send

Mum
Honey I found Weed in Taylors room lets give him a lecture then go smoke it together lol
Hi mum its Taylor, you owe me $20 for that, work it out with dad...
Im just joking I left it on the counter for you
OMG I just told Taylor we smoke weed by accident!!!
Its Taylor again...
Text Message
Send

Mum
So I found something in your room today...
MUM I CAN EXPLAIN. IT'S NOT A MARIJUANA PLANT, IT'S A ROSE WITHOUT THE THORNS AND THE FLOWER
I was talking about your report card?
Oh...
Text Message
Send

FAMILY

Mum

Just got off the phone with your brother

He said you just gave him a boner

Ew mum WTF? That's sick. Why would u say that

boner Amanda

l o a n

Wow mum. You need to learn to text. Yes I gave him £500

Boner

Text Message   Send

Dad
Your mum an I are going to divorce next month
what??? why! call me please?
I wrote Disney and this phone changed it. We are going to Disney.
Text Message
Send

Mum

Where was my 6am text?

I didn't want to wake the sleeping beauty

Me

Mum

3 or 4 bananas, smashed
1/3 cup melted butter
1 cup sugar (can easily reduce to ¾ cup)
1 egg, beaten
1 teaspoon baking soda
Pinch of salt
1 ½ cups of all-purpose flour

what is this a recipe for

why did you wake me up for this

Shut the fuck up

ok goodnight

It's banana bread

Text Message   Send

Mum

Great news – Grandma is homosexual!

Okay?

Homo hot lips

Hot tulips

I am getting fisted now

Frustrated

Grandma is h o m e

from h o s p i t a l

Hahahaa homo hot lips!!??

Text Message | Send

Mum
Hey Honey! You left your phone at home this morning! Just thought I'd let you know.
John? Did you get my message this morning?
Son!? Are you ok???
JOHN!!!
Why are you ignoring your MOTHER!? You are in big trouble!
Oh... wait... I'm an idiot.
Text Message
Send

Mum

How's everything going? Be home soon!

All is well. Just fed and burned the baby three times

BURPED! BURPED THE BABY THREE TIMES!

Text Message

Send

Dad

Honey, you're 20 minutes late, are you ok?

Ok I'm going to look for you.

I called all the hospitals and you aren't in any of them!

YOUR MOTHER IS CRYING

Dad I'm in the bathroom. Calm down.

Oh honey I'm sorry!

Are you doing a period?

Excuse me while I kill myself.

Text Message   Send

Dad

Quick question

Does your hotel have any vasectomies next weekend? Mum and I want to come down.

We have vacancies if that's what you're asking!

Vasectomy on Saturday January 29?

Vacancy!

I'll take it.

Text Message

Send

Dad

Hey honey did you pick up those assholes yet?

I didn't know I was supposed to, dad...

Oh, sh*t wrong number... I meant to send this to your mum.

Oh, okay wait... what assholes?! Are you talking about me and sarah?!

Yes

You're terrible!

Text Message | Send

Dad

Grace, when your mother & I said: Dance through life... we did not mean dance thru college STRIPPING!

You weren't supposed to find out

Well shame on you for dancing where you know Uncle Gary goes to get drunk.

Text Message   Send

Mum

How did you and dad afford a babysitter all the time? They are so expensive!

We didn't we put you guys in the basement and told you there was a tornado... a lot.

That's so messed up. But genius

Text Message   Send

Mum

Mum stop you are not funny. You never make jokes

I made you.

Dad

She hasn't gained that much weight, has she? Do you think we should talk to her about it?

Who are you talking about?

Both I guess. But Jan's weight seems like a normal teenager fluctuation. Libby is starting to worry me, though. What do you think?

Uhhh... I think you're texting the wrong family member! That's what I think!! Oh, and you could stand to lose a few pounds too dad. Maybe you should go on a diet before you start talking about my weight!!!!!!!

please open the door

Text Message   Send

Mum

I've got to tell you something. Are you sitting down?

I am actually. What's up mum?

Your brother was adopted!

What??? What are you talking about?

Why are you telling me this over a text? Call me

Oh this damn phone. I wrote accepted and the phone changed it. He got accepted to Yale!

Text Message   Send

Mum

He broke my heart. Dunno what I'm going to do. I am ruined. I need advice mum.

Honey, Im going to tell you what my mum always told me: If a man breaks your heart, fuck his best friend.

Nana said that?

Text Message   Send

Dad

There's a lizard under my refrigerator.

Sweet. Eat him.

You're helpful.

No charge for the advice.

Text Message | Send

Dad

Dinner 20 mins

What is dinner

Veal and rice. It looks good

Will it poison me?

Let's find out.

If I ever die, and the police are involved... You'll be the first one they question with this attitude.

I'll risk it.

Text Message · Send

Mum

hi mark

grandma's in heaven now

She died??? When? What happened are you ok

yes I'm fine she's in heaven

I understand that but what happened? When?

sorry grandmas

in hairmax hair salon sorry not dead

lol

Text Message   Send

Dad

When u decide u want kids u should adopt so u have something in common with them ha ha ha!!!!!

im joking!!!!! Don't tell ur mum I did that

answer me so I know ur not crying. I watched ur mum have u. Ur mine.

Text Message   Send

FoxyLlama

Hey I was at a party last night and someone went on my phone and changed all the names so who is this? By the sound of it you sound sexy

What's the name??

FoxyLlama

Damn right it is!! ;)

Seriously who it is this?

Your Grandma

Text Message

Send

Mum

I love avocados so much I almost named you avocado

I was going to call you Ava

Or Avo

Text Message

Send

MISCELLANEOUS

Mum

When r u home

By 230 I think

When r u home

By 230 I think

When r u home

By 230 I think

When r u home

STOP

Why r u saying stop

Text Message — Send

Mum

Moonocababa

Best first text ever! Epic!

Nice mum! What does it mean?

Moonocababa

Text Message   Send

Mum

Could you send me Uncle Bill's address?

I cabby found Muir gladness. Canny text nose.

Huh?

I found my glasses!

Text Message   Send

Dad

Heard you got an iPhone, if you need any help with it don't hesitate to call me.
Hope all is well,
Love leon

Hi

AAAAAAAA

WWWWWEW

Don't worry, it takes some time to learn how to text
Practice makes perfect

Oklahoma

Text Message

Send

Mum

Hi mum

Nugget Emily

Nugget

Not nugget

Nugget

????

You're a wreck

Did you do this??

Text Message | Send

Mum

> I havbec6e a new 6ther haven't fukz marpterf the keyboard

You got an iPhone?

> N0 just sent fiqst unassistf text arent you proud

Yes. We need to work on your typing!

Ha ha

> I am on way h6e frm silver moon can you spare some time to improve life

What?!

Text Message   Send

Mum

> Oh dear keepmeupatedas no where riparian wilmslw

If I could understand that, I'd give you a coherent reply.

Text Message — Send

Mum

Btw I looked at the weather for maysville. Looks more like Alaska weather than Georgia or nc. Supposed to snow twice in the next 10 days!

Oops

Sheesh

Kaboom!

I'm no sure if we're just making random noises now or if that was a threat on my life.

Text Message   Send

Mum

I just saw a deer eating a taco!!

Text Message   Send

Mum

I got promiscuous at work!

Don't tell dad lol.

Ha! I was pro moistened.

Got probed

Why is this happening

Pro motionsickness

Oh come on

Lol. Congrats mum!

Text Message

Send

Dad

dan can you give me a ring

my penis is stuck

stuck in the muck

stuck in the butt

what the fuck

What!!!! Just what!!!

Text Message   Send

Mum

Mum did you turn on the air

N wll mayb I did bu I Wnt let u trn it off it to ht

Mum speak English

I m u jrk I m doin wut thy call txt tlk lzr

Did you just call me a lazer?

Mhahahaha nooooo! Loser!

Mum I'm grounding you from texting

Text Message   Send

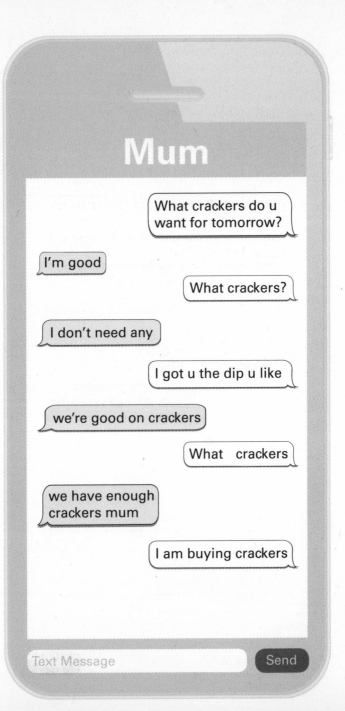

Dad

Jsend to 10 prettiest girls/sweetest guys u knowJ if u don't u will turn ugly in 1 yr.if u get (4) back dang u cute J :* :* :* :*,

Dad what

What?

Did you get 4 back

I got 7 backJ

Text Message   Send

Mum
Mum! I think there's a thief in the house! COME HOME!
Hide in the wardrobe! NOW! I'll be home in 15 minutes!
I can hear steps mum! IM SCARED!
Just be quiet honey!
Okay, I think he's gone now... phew! But I can't get out of the wardrobe! OMG, HE LOCKED ME IN!!
No he didn't, I did. And I came early home from the meeting. Omg, you are easy to scare! PS. Hope you still talking to me! Love you – Mum J
Text Message
Send

Dad
I hate driving you to college its so far
Im sorry dad. Its really only 30 miles away if there was a road going straight to school
You should have taken my advice and gone to Hogwarts for a year and gotten your flying licence. Then you could use a broomstick to get to college
..what?
...filthy mudblood
DAD!
Text Message
Send

WRONG NUMBER

Dad

Night love you

Night

don't even say I love you to your child you know...that's cool too

What?????

Nothing. Goodnight.

I am going to penis rail you when I come to bed

Dad...

Omg

Text Message

Send

Mum
Hey long dong silver. I want to ride the bologna pony tonight!!! You up for the rodeo? ;)
OMG, Mum!!! I'm not coming home tonight...ahhhhhhh!
Oops sorry honey that was meant for ur dad. Just erase that image from your mind.
Text Message
Send

Mum

Mum, apparently I am adopted L

No sweetie ur not I promise J

Honey our son thinks he is adopted, the funny thing is who would want to adopt him hahaha

Wrong person mum =|

...

Text Message   Send

Mum
hey hun, did you get my leather piece, the whip, handcuffs and your g-string? thank god the hubby and the kids are going to be out, tonights going to be great
MUM?! WTF?!
oh, umm... hey Sandra, that was supposed to go to your father J sorry.
but why did you say thankgod the hubbys going out? are cheating on dad?
no um... name your price.
5000 dollars and a laptop and a ipad J
Text Message
Send

Mum
I hear you walking upstairs! Why are you still up?! You're grounded.
From What? L
Bob, what do I ground Alison From? She has no social life/ friends so it's not like taking away any electronics will matter....
Mum! WRONG NUMBER!
Oh sorry hon. You know it's true though.
Text Message
Send

Mum

> Hey hon! I just got Megs present for Christmas! And a sexy Mrs Santa Clause outfit ;) ...And you one too ;)

MUM... EW WTF! THIS IS MEG

> Oh I'm sorry Meg! Santa doesn't exist! :'(I am such a bad parent!

OMG MUM. I KNOW SANTAS NOT REAL THE SECOND PART!

> Oh...did you want a costume too? They're on sale! What size?

OMG MUM.

Text Message | Send

Dad
I think you should wear that pair of dental floss underwear tonight!!!!!
Dad...
That was meant for MUM.
I am so embarrassed. All my friends saw that text and are now laughing at me. FML.
Text Message
Send

Dad
Now that the boys r asleep come on in the bedroom. Your love machine is waiting for u in the new man-thing I bought...
Oh my god dad!!!!!!!!!!
Oh sorry. Thought I was texting your mother
I'm never coming home
If u want I can send a pic
Dear lord no thanks!
Text Message
Send

Dad
Babe, I need you inside me NOW!
I'll be right over!
HA! Busted! you are no longer allowed to date my daughter!
Mr Collins? is this you? I was testing to see if YOUR daughter was too slutty for MY son!
I guess we're on the same track then. Good day to you sir!
Let's try this again next week
Text Message
Send

Dad

Any plans for this evening?

Nothing for early eve – Ideas for later though... ☺

Do I want to know?

Sorry – assumed this was your mother... Dot!!!

There's a thing at the top of the screen that says who you're talking to. It helps if you look.

Text Message

Send